Teaching and Learning
Key Stage 2
Differentiated Activity Book

Letts
EDUCATIONAL

CW00952011

Word

Literacy

Year 3

Contents

 # Introduction

Differentiated Activity Books:

- support the teaching of the Literacy Hour
- help meet the majority of the objectives of the National Literacy Strategy Framework
- contain 30 units of work, sufficient for one school year
- are straightforward and easy to use
- have a clear teaching focus
- contain differentiated activities for each objective at foundation, intermediate and challenging levels of difficulty.

Features of the Word Level Teaching Units

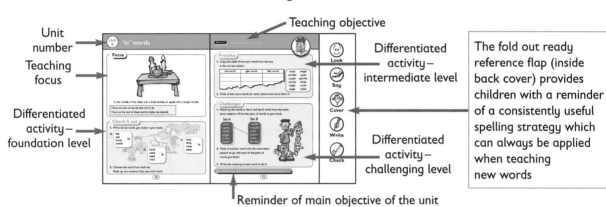

- Unit number
- Teaching focus
- Differentiated activity – foundation level
- Teaching objective
- Differentiated activity – intermediate level
- Differentiated activity – challenging level
- Reminder of main objective of the unit

The fold out ready reference flap (inside back cover) provides children with a reminder of a consistently useful spelling strategy which can always be applied when teaching new words

Using the Differentiated Activity Books

A Variety of Uses

The books may be used to:
- introduce and teach individual National Literacy Strategy Framework objectives independently
- introduce individual National Literacy Strategy Framework objectives prior to studying them during Text Level work
- consolidate, develop and extend National Literacy Strategy Framework objectives studied during Text Level work
- provide work for whole class, group or individual work
- provide work for follow-up homework assignments.

Class Work

The Teaching focus provides a clear explanation of each objective with examples for discussion. Appropriate activities may be chosen from the range of differentiated tasks for discussion, or to work through, with the class.

Group and Individual Work

The Differentiated Activity Books are ideal for group and individual work. Work on the same objective may be realistically matched appropriately to individual children's abilities, allowing children to work independently.

Homework

The material in the books provides an ideal solution to meaningful homework assignments that can be differentiated appropriately for each pupil.

Focus

A **phoneme** is the **smallest unit of sound** in a word. Knowing about phonemes is important for **spelling**.

A phoneme may be made up of **one or more letters** which make **one sound**.

Notice how the three phonemes sound the same.

tw**o** n**ew** sh**oes**

Check it out

Copy the sets of words below. Underline the common phoneme in each set, like the first one.

1. tr<u>ee</u>	f<u>ee</u>t	w<u>ee</u>k	s<u>ee</u>d
2. tea	seat	read	meal
3. rain	paid	mail	wait
4. play	stay	away	day
5. boat	road	foal	loaf
6. show	grow	slow	window
7. moon	pool	food	roof
8. flew	grew	screw	jewel

Practice

1. Complete each word with **oo, ew** or **ue**. Write the words out.

a) s ___ n   c) thr ___   e) bl ___   g) r ___ m

b) fl ___   d) tr ___   f) sch ___ l   h) st ___

2. Complete each word with **oo** or **u**. Write the words out.

a) g ___ d   c) p ___ ll   e) t ___ k   g) b ___ sh

b) l ___ k   d) p ___ sh   f) b ___ ll   h) b ___ k

3. Complete each word with **oi** or **oy**. Write the words out.

a) b ___   c) c ___ n   e) b ___ l   g) destr ___

b) s ___ l   d) j ___   f) p ___ nt   h) enj ___

4. Complete each word with **ow** or **ou**. Write the words out.

a) r ___ nd   c) c ___   e) all ___   g) ab ___ t

b) sh ___ t   d) h ___ l   f) l ___ d   h) t ___ n

5. Complete each word with **or, aw** or **au**. Write the words out.

a) cl ___   c) sp ___ t   e) s ___ cer   g) t ___ ght

b) c ___ ght   d) t ___ n   f) st ___ m   h) str ___

Challenger

Think of and write at least three words for each of the following phonemes:

1. ir (as in b**ir**d)   **5. are** (as in sc**are**)   **9. ea** (as in br**ea**d)

2. ur (as in f**ur**)   **6. ere** (as in th**ere**)   **10. y** (as in fl**y**)

3. er (as in h**er**)   **7. ear** (as in b**ear**)   **11. ar** (as in c**ar**)

4. air (as in f**air**)   **8. ear** (as in f**ear**)   **12. igh** (as in h**igh**)

So – what have you learned about phonemes?

Focus

We can break words down into smaller parts, called **syllables**.
Every syllable must contain at least one **vowel**.

Ro/bots	are	won/der/ful
2 syllables	1 syllable	3 syllables

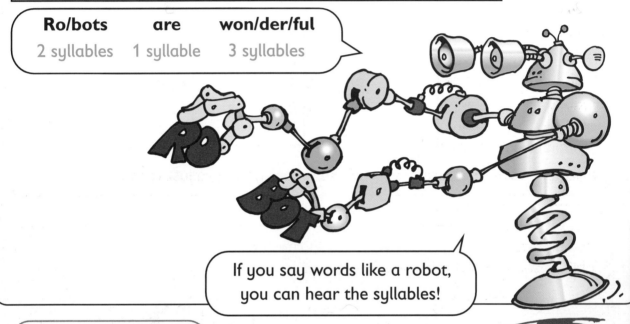

If you say words like a robot,
you can hear the syllables!

Check it out

1. Copy the words below. Say each word slowly. Write if each word has
1 or 2 syllables. Do it like this: **come (1)**

a) runner

b) is

c) because

d) when

e) somewhere

f) school

g) where

h) maybe

i) clock

j) along

k) today

l) going

2. Do the following word sums. Write the two-syllable words you make.

a) dis + gust = _____

b) fun + ny = _____

c) ten + nis = _____

d) par + king = _____

e) but + ton = _____

f) ti + ger = _____

g) mon + key = _____

h) mush + room = _____

Practice

1. Match up the first and second syllables from Sets A and B to make whole
words. Write the words you make in your book.

A	B
den	bit
win	pet
rab	bage
cab	tist
trum	dow

A	B
vil	cil
pen	den
pic	lage
gar	ry
lor	ture

2. Write ten sentences, using each of the words you have just made.

Challenger

1. Think of the last syllable for these words.
Write the words you make in your book.

a) car + a + _____ = _____

b) com + put + _____ = _____

c) e + lec + _____ = _____

d) re + mem + _____ = _____

e) es + tab + _____ = _____

f) to + geth + _____ = _____

g) de + ter + _____ = _____

h) mag + net + _____ = _____

i) mu + sic + _____ = _____

j) won + der + _____ = _____

2. Think of five more words with three syllables and write them down.

So – what have you learned about syllables?

Focus

We can add **ing** to many verbs without changing the spelling of the root word.

walk – walking

bake – baking

If the verb ends with **e** we often drop the **e** when add **ing**.

If the verb ends with a short vowel sound and a consonant, we double the last letter.

hop – hopping

Check it out

Do the following word sums. Write the **ing** words you make in your book.

1. walk + ing = _____
2. wish + ing = _____
3. eat + ing = _____
4. read + ing = _____
5. dream + ing = _____
6. stand + ing = _____

7. paint + ing = _____
8. dress + ing = _____
9. say + ing = _____
10. snow + ing = _____
11. sing + ing = _____
12. hold + ing = _____

Practice

1. Add **ing** to these verbs. Write the new words you make.

a) write

b) ride

c) make

d) hide

e) take

f) fade

g) dine

h) probe

i) rule

2. Write the root word of each verb, like this: **snoring – snore**

a) breathing

b) wiping

c) having

d) waking

e) arriving

f) behaving

g) comparing

h) liking

i) arguing

Challenger

1. Write the sentences below.
Use the correct **ing** form of the verb.

a) I like (bat) better than bowling.

b) The frog is (hop).

c) A poor man was (beg) on the street corner.

d) An old lady is (dig) her garden.

e) The floor is dirty and so it needs (mop).

f) Be careful when you are (cut) paper.

2. These words are all spelled wrongly.
Rewrite them with the correct spelling.

a) invadeing

b) poping

c) sobing

d) bating

e) shapeing

f) slopeing

g) shineing

h) huging

i) snaping

So – what have you learned about adding 'ing' to verbs?

Focus

In the middle of the table was a little bottle, an apple and a single candle.

> There are lots of words that end in **le**.
> The **e** at the end of these words makes **no sound**.

Check it out

1. Write the **le** words you make in your book.

a)
> tab
> cab   le
> humb
> stumb

b)
> hand
> cand   le
> need
> crad

c)
> simp
> dimp   le
> steep
> peop

2. Choose one word from each set.
   Make up one sentence that uses each word.

Practice

1. Copy the table. Write each word from the box
in the correct column.

cle words	**gle** words	**kle** words

uncle	single
twinkle	cycle
jungle	sparkle
article	tickle
angle	circle
eagle	ankle

2. Think of two more words for each column and write them in.

Challenger

1. Match up the words in Set A and Set B which have the same
letter patterns. Write the pairs of words in your book.

Set A
- nibble
- saddle
- muffle
- giggle
- brittle
- dazzle

Set B
- meddle
- snuggle
- sizzle
- bubble
- baffle
- throttle

2. Think of another word with the same letter
pattern to go with each of the pairs of
words you found.

3. Write the meaning of each word in Set A.

So – what have you learned about the letter pattern 'le'?

Focus

A **prefix** is a group of letters we put **in front** of a word (**pre** means **to go in front**).

| happy | **un**happy | obey | **dis**obey |

Prefixes **do not change** the **spelling** of the root word.
Prefixes **do change** the **meaning** of the root word.
The prefixes **un** and **dis** give the word the **opposite** meaning.

Check it out

1. Add the prefixes to make new words. Write the words in your book.

un

a) _____ dress   b) _____ do   c) _____ well   d) _____ fair

dis

a) _____ agree   b) _____ trust   c) _____ place   d) _____ obey

2. Make up two sentences using these two words: **unwell** and **disagree**.

Objectives ~ to recognise and spell common prefixes and how these
influence word meanings
~ to use knowledge of prefixes to generate new words from
root words, especially antonyms

Practice

1. Choose either **un** or **dis** to complete these words.
Write the words in your book. One word uses both **un** and **dis**.
Which one is it?

a) _____ fair   d) _____ cover   g) _____ order

b) _____ trust   e) _____ honest   h) _____ charge

c) _____ pack   f) _____ arm   i) _____ load

2. Write the sentences below. Add a prefix to the underlined word
so that it gives it the opposite meaning.

a) I was feeling quite <u>well</u>.

b) The burglar seemed very <u>honest</u>.

c) When we got home we had to <u>pack</u> our cases.

d) I was <u>able</u> to do all the sums.

e) I <u>agreed</u> with everything that was said.

Challenger

1. Find the eight **un** and **dis** words
in the puzzle.
Write them in your book.

2. Make up one sentence for each
word you found.

3. Now write the opposite of each
word you found in the puzzle.

a	b	c	d	i	s	a	b	l	e	f	g
x	c	v	b	n	m	u	n	b	o	l	t
u	n	w	r	a	p	q	w	r	t	y	e
d	g	d	i	s	o	r	d	e	r	h	k
h	z	x	d	i	s	a	r	m	b	v	c
m	n	b	u	n	b	u	c	k	l	e	v
w	d	i	s	o	w	n	g	f	h	d	k
q	u	o	k	u	n	f	a	s	t	e	n

So – what have you learned about the prefixes 'un' and 'dis'?

13

Focus

A **prefix** is a **group of letters** that comes **at the beginning** of a word.
If we know what the prefix means it can help us understand some words better.

refill

depart

prefix

re often means **again**.	**de** often means **away from**.	**pre** often means **before** or **in front of**.

Check it out

1. Match each word with its meaning. Write them in your book.

return   to pay back again

repay   to fill again

renew   to come back again

refill   to play again

reconsider   to make new again

replay   to consider again

2. Add the prefix **re** to these words and write them in your book.

a) ____ place   b) ____ form   c) ____ trace   d) ____ call

Objectives ~ to recognise and spell common prefixes
~ to understand how these influence word meanings
~ to use the term prefix

Practice

1. Choose the prefix **de** and/or **pre** to complete each word. Use a dictionary if you are not sure. Write the words in your book.

a) _____ part

b) _____ fix

c) _____ heat

d) _____ historic

e) _____ face

f) _____ port

g) _____ frost

h) _____ caution

i) _____ mature

j) _____ posit

k) _____ press

l) _____ arrange

2. Choose three **de** and three **pre** words from those you have just made.
Write a sentence for each word to show you understand what each means.

Challenger

1. Copy the table below. Write each word from the box in the correct column.

prevent	demolish	refresh
preposition	recite	deduct
decay	reassure	precede

re words	**de** words	**pre** words

2. Use a dictionary to write one more word in each column.

3. Choose two words from each group. Write what they mean.

So – what have you learned about the prefixes 're', 'de' and 'pre'?

Focus

When we study **other subjects** and **read different sorts of books,** we always come across **new and interesting words**.

transport
cars, lorries, yachts, submarines

food
pizza, curry, biscuits rice, hamburgers

We can put words into **different sets**.

biscuits
cars
curry
hamburgers
lorries
pizza
rice
submarines
yachts

We can put words in **alphabetical order.**

pizza
a flat round of dough covered with a savoury mixture of tomatoes and cheese, etc. and baked in an oven.

We can write **definitions** for each word.

Check it out

1. Copy the table. Put each word from the box in the correct column.

cook	triangle	baker	rounders	cube
nurse	rugby	rectangle	cricket	square
football	circle	farmer	swimming	teacher

Sports	Jobs	Mathematical shapes
rounders		

Practice

1. Use the table you completed in the 'Check it out' section.
   Write the list of things from each column again.
   But this time, write them in alphabetical order.

2. Match up the name of each shape in A with its definition in B.
   Write down the name of each shape and its definition.

A

triangle

cube

rectangle

square

circle

B

1. a round flat shape
2. a solid object with six equal square surfaces
3. a four-sided shape with opposite sides of equal length, and four right angles
4. a shape with four sides of the same length and four corners, each with a right angle
5. a shape with three straight lines and three angles

Challenger

1. Divide these words into two sets. Write each set in alphabetical order.

history	astronaut	geography	atmosphere
technology	satellite	universe	science
gravity	English	planet	mathematics

2. Choose one of the sets of words. Make up a definition for each word.
   Use a dictionary to help.

So – what have you learned about collecting words?

Focus

We can often guess the meaning of a word from the **context** in which it appears (from the meanings of words and the pictures around it).

The man was asleep in a **hammock**.

We can tell a hammock is a kind of bed:
a) by the picture
b) by the words in the rest of the sentence.

Check it out

Choose the best word from the box to fill each gap.
Look for the clues in the sentences and write them out.

(sentry   hobby   saddle   camera   honest   lizard)

1. I took the photo with my c_____ .

2. My h_____ is collecting stamps.

3. A l_____ has a long tail.

4. The jockey put the s_____ on the horse.

5. The s_____ was on guard during the night.

6. I never tell lies because I am h_____ .

Practice

Write the correct meaning for each underlined word.
Use a dictionary to help.

1. The ship <u>capsized</u> in the storm.
a) overturned   b) flew

2. The <u>orchids</u> gave off a lovely smell.
a) white flowers   b) fruit trees

3. The <u>astronomer</u> looks through the telescope.
a) He flies in a rocket.   b) He studies the stars.

4. The <u>limpet</u> clung to the rock.
a) a sailor   b) a small shellfish

5. The <u>colt</u> ran quickly behind the mare.
a) a young male horse   b) a thief

6. There was a <u>pheasant</u> in the field.
a) a poor country person   b) a type of bird

Challenger

Write what you think the underlined words in these sentences mean.
Use a dictionary to help.

1. The <u>canary</u> sang loudly.
2. The ship appeared on the <u>horizon</u>.
3. The pilot shut the <u>hangar</u> door.
4. The barge moved along the <u>canal</u>.

5. I bought a paper from a <u>kiosk</u>.
6 A <u>shoal</u> of fish swam past.
7. A <u>kid</u> was eating grass in a field.
8. The child used an <u>abacus</u> to count.

So – what have you learned about using context?

Focus

A **dictionary** can help you find the **meanings** of words and help you with their **spellings**.

jam → jewel → jigsaw → joke → jungle

These words are in alphabetical order.
The words in a **dictionary** are arranged in **alphabetical order**.
Each word in a dictionary has a **definition** which tells you the **meaning** of the word.

jam   a sweet food made by cooking fruit with sugar

Check it out

Write the answers to these questions in your book.

1. How can a dictionary help you?

2. In what order are the words in a dictionary written?

3. Write these words in alphabetical order:

   jungle   jewel   jam   joke   jigsaw

4. Write the definition of **jam**.

5. Check the spelling of these words. Write them correctly.

a) jowke   b) jungel   c) jigsore   d) jewell

6. Look up the meaning of the words in question 5 in your dictionary.
   Write a definition for each word.

Objectives ~ to have a secure understanding of the purpose and
organisation of dictionaries
~ to use dictionaries to learn or check the spellings and
definitions of words

Practice

1. Use a dictionary to look up and write the definitions of the words below.
   They come in the first quarter of your dictionary (a–e).

a) arrow   b) barn   c) diamond

2. Look up and write the definitions of the words below.
   They come in the second quarter of your dictionary (f–m).

a) gorilla   b) kilt   c) million

3. Look up and write the definitions of the words below.
   They come in the third quarter of your dictionary (n–r).

a) orchard   b) plaice   c) rye

4. Look up and write the definitions of the words below.
   They come in the last quarter of your dictionary (s–z).

a) snorkel   b) unicorn   c) yarn

Challenger

1. Use a dictionary to answer these riddles.
a) My name begins with **add**. I am a snake.
b) My name begins with **cl**. You find and eat me near the sea.
c) My name begins with **j**. I ride fast horses.
d) My name begins with **m**. I cover your face to hide it.
e) My name begins with **sl**. You wear me indoors.

2. Check the spelling of these words in a dictionary. Rewrite them correctly.
a) garadge   c) musium   e) theater
b) restaraunt   d) hopsitel   f) librery

So – what have you learned about dictionaries?

Focus

Synonyms are words which have the **same** or **very similar meanings**. Using synonyms makes our writing more **interesting** and **adds variety**.

wet – damp

Check it out

Join up the the synonyms. Write the pairs of words in your book.

1.

big	enjoy
little	excellent
like	large
good	leave
go	small

2.

nice	plump
nasty	pleasant
fat	giggle
call	horrible
laugh	shout

Practice

Copy each set of words below. Underline the odd one out.
Say why it is the odd one out.

1. new   fresh   dirty   modern

2. come   garden   reach   arrive

3. cork   dig   scoop   shovel

4. home   house   dwelling   pencil

5. kick   jump   leap   bound

6. animals   people   persons   folk

7. push   shove   give   thrust

8. see   catch   observe   behold

Challenger

Think of a suitable synonym to replace each underlined word.
Write your new sentences in your book.

1. The children <u>ran</u> towards the beach.

2. The thief <u>took</u> the jewels and escaped.

3. There are <u>many</u> things I would like.

4. The contest <u>began</u> at three o'clock.

5. My sister's bedroom is always <u>tidy</u>.

6. I was <u>sure</u> I was right.

7. We had to <u>pull</u> the boat out of the water.

8. I was digging with an old <u>spade</u>.

So – what have you learned about synonyms?

Focus

These are the **key** words.

These words have the **same** or **similar** meanings to the key words. They are **synonyms**.

This is a page from my thesaurus.

nag	pester, annoy, worry
nap	sleep, doze, snooze
naughty	bad, disobedient, unruly
neat	clean, orderly, tidy
nibble	bite, chew, gnaw
noise	uproar, din, racket

The words in a **thesaurus** are arranged in **alphabetical order**. A thesaurus can help you find words with the **same** or **similar** meanings (**synonyms**).

Check it out

Use the page from the 'Focus' section and the thesaurus above to answer these questions.

1. In what order are words in a thesaurus arranged?

2. How does a thesaurus help you?

3. Write a word that has a similar meaning to:

a) nag   b) nibble   c) noise

4. Write some synonyms for:

a) neat   b) naughty   c) nap

Practice

Use a thesaurus to find a synonym for each of these words:

1. add
2. close
3. evil
4. heap

5. keen
6. merry
7. odd
8. pole

9. repeat
10. stare
11. walk
12. zero

Challenger

Rewrite the sentences. Replace each underlined word with
a suitable synonym. Use a thesaurus to help.

1. I gave the nail a <u>blow</u> with the hammer.
2. It is very <u>dangerous</u> to swim in the sea in a storm.
3. There was a <u>gap</u> between the floorboards.
4. The child <u>munched</u> the crisps loudly.
5. There was a nasty <u>odour</u> coming from the dustbin.
6. The plane made a <u>perfect</u> landing.
7. When the teacher entered the children were <u>quiet</u>.
8. I was <u>tired</u> after the long walk.

So – what have you learned about a thesaurus?

Focus

When we write **dialogue** (the things people say), we sometimes use the word **said** too often. There are many other **dialogue words** we can use instead.

Am I on the right road to London?

No. You need to go left at the next turning.

"Am I on the right road to London?" the driver said (asked).

"No. You need to go left at the next turning," said (replied) the farmer.

Check it out

Copy these sentences. Underline the dialogue word in each, like the first one.

1. "Let's go swimming!" the child <u>shouted</u>.
2. "Where is my pen?" the boy asked.
3. "Look out!" yelled the girl.
4. "What a lovely picture!" the teacher exclaimed.
5. "Please walk quietly," the guide whispered.
6. "I didn't do my homework," the boy mumbled.
7. "It's very funny," the clown giggled.
8. "I've hurt my toe!" the lady cried.

Objectives ~ to recognose common vocabulary for introducing and
concluding dialogue
~ to collect synonyms useful when writing dialogue

Practice

Copy these sets of dialogue words.

Underline the odd word out in each set, like the first one.

Say why they are the odd ones out.

1.	<u>whisper</u>	call	shout
2.	ask	request	explain
3.	mumble	mutter	scream
4.	moan	giggle	groan
5.	beg	reply	answer
6.	whisper	murmur	howl
7.	screech	sigh	shriek
8.	grumble	complain	stutter

Challenger

Copy out this passage. Think of a suitable dialogue word for each
gap. Do not use the word **said** at all.

"Is it time to get ready?" Ben _____ his mum.

"No, not yet," she _____ .

"It's too long to wait!" Emma _____ .

"Don't worry. The time will soon go," Mum _____ .

"Look! Someone is coming!" Ben _____ .

"Try not to shout or you'll wake the baby," Mum _____ .

"Sorry," Ben _____ .

"I think it's Dan," Emma _____ .

"You like him, don't you?" Ben _____ .

"No, I do not!" Emma _____ .

So – what have you learned about dialogue words?

Focus

A **suffix** is a group of letters we add to the **end** of a word.

Suffixes **change the meaning** of the word.

When we compare adjectives, we often add the suffixes **er** and **est**.

Many adjectives can add **er** and **est** without any change to the spelling of the root word.

small   smaller   smallest

When an adjective ends in **e**, we drop the **e** when we add **er** or **est**.

brave   braver   bravest

When the adjective ends with **y**, we change the **y** to **i** and add the **er** or **est**.

heavy   heavier   heaviest

Check it out

1. Copy and complete this table.

Root adjective	Add **er**	Add **est**
tall	taller	
bright		brightest
	smoother	
narrow		
		oldest
sweet		
	longer	
		roughest

Practice

Add **er** and **est** to each adjective. Do it like this: **large – larger – largest**

1. busy　　　　**5.** tame　　　　**9.** cute

2. healthy　　**6.** noisy　　　**10.** nice

3. safe　　　　**7.** lucky　　　**11.** pretty

4. pale　　　　**8.** ripe　　　　**12.** sturdy

Challenger

1. Find and circle ten **er** and **est**
words in this puzzle.
Write them in your book.

a	b	c	n	o	i	s	i	e	r	d	e
d	i	r	t	i	e	s	t	h	j	k	n
z	x	c	v	b	w	i	d	e	s	t	v
q	w	e	r	c	o	l	d	e	r	t	y
d	c	l	e	v	e	r	e	s	t	s	x
o	p	j	s	t	r	a	n	g	e	r	p
g	h	s	i	l	l	i	e	s	t	v	c
t	r	y	n	i	c	e	r	b	c	h	u
p	r	e	t	t	i	e	s	t	f	c	x
b	f	h	g	t	r	h	i	g	h	e	r

2. Now write each adjective you have found without its suffix.
Do it like this: **noisier – noise**

So – what have you learned about the suffixes 'er' and 'est' ?

Focus

A **suffix** is a group of letters we add to the **end** of a word. Suffixes **change the meaning** of the word.

Rule 1: We can add **y** to many words without any change to the spelling of the root word.

crunch – crunchy

noise – noisy

Rule 2: When a word ends in **e** we often drop the **e** when we add **y**.

Rule 3: If the word ends with a short vowel sound and a consonant, we double the last letter.

sun – sunny

Check it out

Copy and complete the sentences below. Add **y** to the words in the brackets.

1. The nail was very (rust).
2. I feel very (sleep).
3. I do not like (greed) people.
4. The road was very (twist).
5. The boy was very (craft).
6. My bedroom is rather (mess).
7. It is (frost) today.
8. There was an (oil) patch on the ground.
9. The plug was (fault).
10. My lettuce is nice and (crisp).

Practice

1. Add the suffix **y** to each word below. Write the words in your book.

a) noise   d) stripe   g) scare

b) ice   e) grime   h) doze

c) stone   f) shade   i) ease

2. Make up one sentence for each of the new words you have made.

Challenger

1. Copy each word below and write the word from which
it came (its root). Do it like this: **funny – fun**

a) fatty   f) pippy

b) nutty   g) sunny

c) dotty   h) jammy

d) saggy   i) starry

e) ratty   j) puppy

2. Copy the words below. After each word, say if it follows Rule 1, 2 or 3 in
the 'Focus' section. Do it like this: **scary (Rule 2)**

a) noisy   d) puppy   g) dusty

b) springy   e) scaly   h) tabby

c) slimy   f) daddy   i) fishy

So – what have you learned about the suffix 'y'?

Focus

Singular means one. **Plural** means more than one.

We add **s** to many singular nouns to make them plural.

One book.

Lots of book**s**.

If the singular noun ends with **s**, **sh**, **ch** or **x**, we add **es** to make it plural.

One box.

Lots of box**es.**

If the singular noun ends with a consonant **+ y** we change the **y** to **i** and add **es**.

One baby.

Lots of bab**ies.**

Check it out

1. Copy and complete the tables below. Write the singular or plural.

Singular	Plural
table	tables
chair	
door	
stool	
mirror	
bed	

Singular	Plural
	pots
	forks
	plates
	windows
	mats
	carpets

Objectives ~ to investigate and identify basic rules for changing
nouns when s is added
~ to use the terms 'singular' and 'plural' appropriately

Practice

Copy and insert the correct plural in each gap.

1. one fox – a family of _____

2. one city – two _____

3. one church – many _____

4. one berry – a basket of _____

5. one brush – five _____

6. one pony – ten _____

7. one lady – several _____

8. one bush – lots of _____

9. one copy – three _____

10. one fly – a swarm of _____

11. one glass – a few _____

12. one arch – a row of _____

Challenger

Rewrite the sentences below. Change the underlined nouns into their plural form.
Make any other changes necessary so the sentences make sense.

1. The <u>fox</u> hid in the <u>bush</u>.

2. The <u>lady</u> pushed the <u>baby</u> in the <u>pram</u>.

3. The <u>girl</u> had a <u>diary</u>.

4. Put the <u>glass</u> in the <u>box</u>.

5. A <u>poppy</u> is a <u>flower</u>.

6. The <u>driver</u> of the <u>lorry</u> was tired.

7. I washed the <u>brush</u> after I painted the <u>picture</u>.

8. The <u>boy</u> could not solve the <u>mystery</u>.

So – what have you learned about singular and plural nouns?

Focus

Singular means one. **Plural** means more than one.

If the singular noun ends with a vowel **+ y**, we add an **s** to make it plural.

One monkey.   Lots of monkey**s**.

If the singular noun ends with **f**, we often change the **f** to **v** and add **es** to make it plural.

One loaf.   Lots of loa**ves**.

If the singular noun ends with **o**, we often add **es** to make it plural.

One potato.   Lots of potato**es**.

Check it out

1. Copy and complete the tables below. Write the singular or plural.

Singular	Plural
key	keys
day	
toy	
guy	
bay	
turkey	

Singular	Plural
	journeys
	jockeys
	donkeys
	trolleys
	chimneys
	holidays

Practice

Copy and insert the correct plural in each gap.

1. one leaf – lots of _____

2. one tomato – two _____

3. one hero – many _____

4. one volcano – six _____

5. one wolf – a pack of _____

6. one calf – ten _____

7. one shelf – several _____

8. one potato – a sack of _____

9. one thief – three _____

10. one half – two _____

11. one echo – lots of _____

12. one cargo – many _____

Challenger

Rewrite the sentences below. Change the underlined nouns into their plural form. Make any other changes necessary so the sentences make sense.

1. The <u>wolf</u> escaped when the <u>volcano</u> began to blow.

2. The <u>thief</u> stole the <u>key</u> to the house.

3. The <u>monkey</u> jumped over the <u>donkey</u>.

4. The baker put the <u>loaf</u> on the <u>shelf</u>.

5. Put the <u>potato</u> and <u>tomato</u> on the <u>trolley</u>.

6. The <u>calf</u> was frightened by the sound of the <u>echo</u>.

7. The <u>boy</u> tried to catch the <u>leaf</u>.

8. The <u>cargo</u> was lifted out of the ships' <u>hold</u>.

So – what have you learned about singular and plural nouns?

Focus

Some words contain **silent letters**. We cannot hear these letters in some words when we say them.

knot   **w**rist   **g**nome

Try saying the words exactly as they are spelled and see how funny they sound!

Check it out

1. Copy the table below. Write the words from the box into the correct columns.

knot	wrap	wreck	gnat	gnome
wrong	know	gnaw	knee	gnash
gnarl	write	wrist	knife	knock

Silent **w**	Silent **k**	Silent **g**
wrap		

2. Write out the three sets of words again. Underline the silent letter in each word.

Practice

1. Match up each word with its definition.

Write them in your book.

wrist	to destroy or ruin
write	this joins your hand to your arm
wrong	a leg joint
wreck	to hit or bump
knot	something you do with a pen
knee	you cut with this
knife	the opposite of right
knock	where two pieces of string are tied

2. Use a dictionary to write a definition for:

gnat, gnash, gnaw, gnome and **gnarled**

Challenger

1. Sort the words in the box into three 'silent letter' sets.

knuckle	sign	wrestle	knack	align	wriggle
reign	wrinkle	knight	answer	knit	resign

2. Use the words from the box above to work out these words.

Write the words.

a) _ _ g _

b) r _ _ g _

c) k _ _ t

d) k _ a _ _ _

e) w _ _ g g _ _

f) w _ _ _ _ k l e

g) a _ _ g _

h) r e _ _ g _

i) k _ i _ _ _ _

j) k _ _ _ _ _ _ _

k) w _ _ _ s t _ _ _

l) _ _ _ _ w _ _ _

So – what have you learned about silent letters?

Focus

Some words contain **silent letters**. We cannot hear these letters in some words when we say them.

| lam**b** | ta**l**k | lis**t**en |

Try saying the words exactly as they are spelled and see how funny they sound!

Check it out

1. Copy the table below. Write the words from the box into the correct columns.

comb	climb	talk	listen	thumb
palm	crumb	rustle	half	calf
calm	chalk	glisten	lamb	bustle

Silent **b**	Silent **l**	Silent **t**
comb		

2. Write out the three sets of words again. Underline the silent letter in each word.

Practice

1. Match up each word with its definition.
Write them in your book.

lamb	like a small finger
comb	to speak
thumb	a young sheep
crumb	soft white rock you can write with
talk	a young cow
palm	a small piece of bread or cake
calf	this keeps your hair tidy
chalk	a type of tree

2. Use a dictionary to write a definition for:

rustle, listen, glisten and **bustle**

Challenger

1. Write the words in the box in three 'silent letter' sets.

limb	stalk	moisten	yolk	hasten	folk
numb	fasten	walk	plumber	debt	castle

2. Use the words from the box above to work out these words.

a) l __ __ b

b) __ __ __ __ b __ __

c) __ __ __ __ l __

d) w __ l __

e) __ o i __ t __ __

f) f __ __ t __ __

g) n __ __ b

h) __ __ b __

i) y __ l __

j) f __ l __

k) h __ __ t __ __

l) __ __ __ t l e

So – what have you learned about silent letters?

Focus

A **compound word** is made up of two shorter words which have been joined together.

 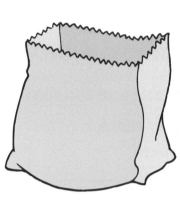 

hand   +   bag   =   handbag

Check it out

1. Do these word sums. Write the answers in your book.

a) butter + fly = _____

b) sun + shine = _____

c) sea + side = _____

d) sheep + dog = _____

e) pan + cake = _____

f) horse + shoe = _____

g) play + time = _____

h) tooth + brush = _____

i) bed + room = _____

j) grand + father = _____

k) farm + yard = _____

l) foot + ball = _____

2. Choose five of the compound words you have just made.
Make up one sentence containing each word.

Practice

1. Match up pairs of words to make compound words.
   Write the pairs of words in your book.

run	shake
snow	day
hand	way
table	bow
birth	paper
post	ball
wall	cloth
rain	card

2. Now write the words you have just made in alphabetical order.

Challenger

1. Add a suitable word to each of the words below to form a compound word.
   You may add a word at the beginning or end of each word.

a) motor   e) ball   i) gentle

b) wall   f) after   j) under

c) tea   g) fire   k) moon

d) door   h) paste   l) head

2. Write as many compound words as possible that begin with:

a) some   b) any   c) no

So – what have you learned about compound words?

Focus

A **suffix** is a group of letters we add to the **end** of a word.

Suffixes **change the meaning** of the word.

We can change some **nouns** into **adjectives** by adding the suffixes **ful** or **less**.

careful

careless

Careful really means **full of care**. When **ful** comes at the end of a word, it only has one **l**.

The suffix **less** at the end of a word gives the word its opposite meaning.

Check it out

1. Copy this table and fill in the missing words.

Root word	+ suffix **ful**	+ suffix **less**
hope	hopeful	hopeless
pain		
use		
power		
help		
cheer		
harm		
colour		
thank		
thought		

Practice

Rewrite the sentences below. Change the suffixes of the underlined
words to give them the opposite meaning.

1. The children were very <u>careful</u> with the paint.

2. The injection was <u>painless</u>.

3. The new pen I bought turned out to be <u>useful</u>.

4. The words I spoke were very <u>thoughtless</u>.

5. I spent a very <u>restful</u> night in the new bed.

6. It was a very <u>cheerful</u> and <u>colourful</u> scene.

7. The liquid in the bottle was <u>harmless</u>.

8. I felt strangely <u>powerful</u> when I scored a goal.

Challenger

1. What is the root word of each of these?
Do it like this: **beautiful – beauty**

a) merciless   b) plentiful   c) pitiless   d) dutiful

2. Choose either **ful** or **less** to complete these. Write the words in your book.
One word can take both suffixes. Which word is it?

a) end   d) deceit   g) noise
b) wonder   e) heart   h) blame
c) speech   f) skill   i) mind

3. Make up one sentence for each of the words you made in question 2.

So – what have you learned about the suffixes 'ful' and 'less'?

Suffixes 4: 'ly'

Focus

A **suffix** is a group of letters we add to the end of a word.
Suffixes **change the meaning** of the word.
We can change some **adjectives** into **adverbs** by adding the suffixes **ly**.

We can add the suffix **ly** to many adjectives without changing the spelling of the root word.

The lady drove **quickly** and **carefully**.
(quick)   (careful)

The poor girl cried **miserably**.
(miserable)

When the adjective ends in **e**, we drop the **e** before adding the suffix **ly**.

When the adjective ends in a consonant **+ y**, we change the **y** to **i** before adding the suffix **ly**.

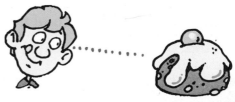

The man looked at the cake **hungrily**.
(hungry)

Check it out

Add the suffix **ly** to the words below. Write the words in your book.

1. sweet
2. fair
3. clever
4. proud
5. quick
6. hopeful
7. cheap
8. equal
9. plain
10. truthful
11. poor
12. loyal

Practice

Rewrite the sentences below. Change the underlined adjectives into adverbs by adding the suffix **ly**. The first one has been done for you.

1. The man shouted <u>angry</u>.
   The man shouted angrily.
2. The children chattered <u>noisy</u>.
3. The girl did everything <u>sensible</u>.
4. I did the spellings <u>easy</u>.
5. The doctor lifted the baby <u>gentle</u>.
6. The girl smiled <u>pretty</u>.
7. The waiter spilled the soup <u>clumsy</u>.
8. The old man sat down <u>weary</u>.
9. The injured child called <u>feeble</u>.
10. The knight knelt <u>humble</u> in front of the king.

Challenger

1. Write the adjective from which each adverb below comes.
   Do it like this: **distinctly – distinct**

   a) merrily   d) horribly   g) accidentally
   b) steadily   e) comfortably   h) thankfully
   c) heavily   f) simply   i) patiently

2. Make up some sentences using each of the adverbs in question 1 correctly.

So – what have you learned about the suffix 'ly'?

Focus

When we speak or write, we sometimes **shorten** words by **missing out some letters**. These words are called **contractions**. (To contract means to make smaller.)

Don't do that!

do not – don't

We use an **apostrophe** to show where letters are missing.

Check it out

1. Match up each contraction with its longer form and write them in your book.
Do it like this: **isn't – is not**

isn't	does not
wasn't	you are
doesn't	we would
she's	is not
it's	we will
you're	was not
I've	it is
we'll	I am
I'm	she is
we'd	I have

Practice

1. Rewrite these contractions in your book. Put in the missing apostrophes.

a) hasnt   f) cant   k) werent   p) wouldnt

b) theres   g) whos   l) thats   q) hows

c) theyre   h) were   m) youve   r) theyve

d) Ill   i) shell   n) theyll   s) itll

e) theyd   j) shed   o) wed   t) Im

2. Now write what each contraction stands for.

Do it like this: **hasn't – has not**

Challenger

Rewrite the following sentences.

Write a contraction for each of the underlined words.

1. You <u>should not</u> eat toadstools.

2. We <u>did not</u> do it.

3. <u>You are</u> my best friend.

4. <u>He will</u> regret his actions.

5. I <u>can not</u> lift the heavy box.

6. <u>I would</u> go if I could.

7. <u>It is</u> a lovely picture.

8. <u>They are</u> my favourite sweets.

9. The lady <u>does not</u> have a car.

10. I <u>do not</u> think <u>I will</u> be able to come.

So – what have you learned about
using an apostrophe in contractions?

Focus

Definitions are the **meanings given to words**.
Definitions need to be **precise** and **accurate**.

You will find definitions for most words in a **dictionary**.
Sometimes the same word may have **more than one meaning**.

hunt 1. (verb) Animals hunt other animals for food; people hunt animals for food and fur, and some hunt for sport.

2. (noun) A hunt is a group of people who meet together to hunt animals.

3. (verb) If you hunt for something, you look for it because you have lost it.

hurdle 1. (noun) A hurdle is a kind of fence used for jumps in horse racing.

2. (noun) A hurdle is a difficulty that you have to overcome in order to do or gain something.

Check it out

1. How many definitions do the following words have in the dictionary above:

a) hunt   b) hurdle?

2. Write the two definitions for **hunt** that are verbs.

3. Which word means:

a) a kind of fence used for jumping over?

b) a group of people who meet together to hunt animals?

c) a difficulty you have to overcome?

d) to look for something because you have lost it?

Practice

There are three definitions for each word below. One definition is false.

Write each word and its two correct definitions.

(Use a dictionary if you are unsure.)

1. bow
a) a curved piece of wood for shooting arrows
b) the lowest part of something
c) a decorative knot in ribbon or string

2. work
a) hair growing on sheep used for making clothes
b) the activity people do to earn a living
c) a task or duty you have to do

3. scrape
a) to take off some of the surface with a sharp object
b) a mark on an object
c) a line of stitches joining two pieces of cloth

4. firm
a) fire
b) something that feels solid
c) when someone means what they say

5. crook
a) something brittle and hard
b) is the inside of your elbow
c) someone who is dishonest or a criminal

Challenger

1. Write one more definition for each of the words in the 'Practice' section.

2. Write two definitions for each of the following words.
Use a dictionary to help you.
a) brand
b) grate
c) dart
d) mine
e) fan
f) seal

So – what have you learned about definitions?

Focus

Many **books** are arranged in **alphabetical order,** e.g. dictionaries and thesauruses.

anorak   **b**elt   **c**ap   **d**ress

These words are organised in **alphabetical order** according to their **first** letter.

s**a**ndals   s**c**arf   s**h**irt   s**o**cks

These words all begin with the same letter so they are organised in **alphabetical order** according to their **second** letter.

Check it out

1. In the alphabet, write the letter which comes after each of these.

a) n   b) p   c) j   d) s   e) h

2. Write the letter which comes before each of these.

a) c   b) o   c) g   d) v   e) t

3. Write the letter which comes between each of these.

a) **b** and **d**   b) **h** and **j**   c) **l** and **n**   d) **o** and **q**   e) **v** and **x**

4. Write these words in alphabetical order.

a) cage   ant   dance   bird   b) nail   prince   melon   oil

Practice

Write these words in alphabetical order, according to their second letter.

1. eagle   eye   egg   elephant
2. deer   day   dinner   drum
3. pigeon   parrot   peacock   pheasant
4. wood   wrist   west   winter
5. lunch   leave   liner   locker
6. fog   frog   fall   flag
7. bucket   bell   band   bin
8. shine   skid   sit   send

Challenger

1. Write the days of the week in alphabetical order.

2. Think of three:

a) children's names beginning with **M**.
b) countries beginning with **B**.
c) towns beginning with **L**.
d) animals beginning with **H**.
e) parts of the body beginning with **E**.

Write each list in alphabetical order in your book.

3. Think of a word that could come between each of the following in a dictionary:

a) **magic** and **milk**   c) **petal** and **pull**
b) **saddle** and **sing**   d) **tile** and **trail**

So – what have you learned about alphabetical order?

Opposites

Focus

Words that are **opposite** are as **different in meaning as possible**.

This car is **new** but that car is **old**.

Check it out

Choose a word from the box that is opposite to the words numbered below. Write the answers in your book like this: **big – small**

high	quiet	hard	small	tame	sell
dry	cold	smooth	full	wrong	go

1. big   **4.** right   **7.** noisy   **10.** rough

2. come   **5.** buy   **8.** low   **11.** empty

3. wild   **6.** hot   **9.** easy   **12.** wet

Practice

Rewrite these sentences in your book. Change the underlined words to words with the opposite meaning.

1. It was a <u>fat</u> cucumber.
2. The train went very <u>slowly</u>.
3. My glass was <u>empty</u>.
4. The dog jumped over the <u>high</u> wall.
5. The questions were <u>difficult</u>.
6. The weather was <u>hot</u> and <u>dry</u>.
7. The <u>twisty</u> road was very <u>long</u>.
8. The <u>tall</u> man entered the room.

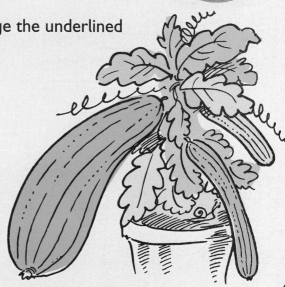

Challenger

Copy the words below. Find the word in each set that is the opposite to the word on the left. Circle the opposite word, like the first one.

1. **heavy**   tall   (light)   thin
2. **strong**   weak   long   small
3. **found**   made   went   lost
4. **enemy**   friend   child   toy
5. **upper**   middle   behind   lower
6. **rude**   noisy   polite   tiny
7. **blunt**   bad   heavy   sharp
8. **bitter**   sweet   bent   smelly
9. **happy**   joyful   sad   best
10. **wide**   narrow   enormous   near

So – what have you learned about opposites?

Focus

You can sometimes find **smaller words** 'hiding' **in longer words**!
Spotting them can often help you to remember the **spelling** of the longer word.

A **pie**ce of **pie**.   An **island** – **is land** surrounded by water!

Check it out

1. Copy these sets of words. Underline the small word hiding in each.

Do it like this: **here**   w<u>here</u>   t<u>here</u>

a) **the**   them   then   there   they   these   their
b) **hen**   when   then
c) **who**   whose   whole
d) **other**   mother   brother   another
e) **in**   win   drink   indoors   pinch   prince

2. Write all the small words you can find in each of the words below.

a) because   c) sometime   e) anywhere
b) everybody   d) nothing   f) weather

Practice

Make some new words. Underline the small word that is the same in each
of the new words you have made. The first one has been done for you.

1. Change the **b** in **bend** to **l, m, s, t, fri**.
   <u>le</u>nd, m<u>en</u>d, s<u>en</u>d, t<u>en</u>d, fri<u>en</u>d

2. Change the **n** in **nice** to **m, tw, off, pol**.

3. Change the **c** in **cape** to **g, t, dr, gr, sh**.

4. Change the **b** in **band** to **h, l, s, w, br, st**.

5. Change the **c** in **care** to **d, h, r, sh, sc, sp**.

6. Change the **h** in **harm** to **f, w, ch, al**.

7. Change the **n** in **near** to **h, f, p, y, w, b**.

8. Change the **c** in **cage** to **p, r, w, st, vill**.

Challenger

1. Do these word puzzles and write the word you are left with.
   The first one has been done for you.

a) Take **ear** out of **feared**.
   (You are left with **fed**.)

b) Take the **art** out of **starting**.

c) Take the **one** out of **money**.

d) Take the **all** out of **shallow**.

e) Take the **now** out of **snowing**.

f) Take the **owl** out of **slowly**.

g) Take the **act** out of **practice**.

2. Write as many words as you can that contain each of these smaller words:

a) owl
b) ark
c) our
d) port
e) urn
f) one
g) use
h) ink

**So – what have you learned about looking
for small words in longer words?**

Focus

A **prefix** is a **group of letters** that comes **at the beginning** of a word.
If we know what the prefix means, it can help us to understand some words better.

misbehave

exhausted

| **mis** often means **wrongly** or **badly**. | **ex** often means **out of** or **away from**. |

Check it out

1. Match up each word with its correct definition. Write the answers in your book.

misspell	to handle a situation badly
misbehave	to use something badly
misjudge	to make a spelling mistake
mishandle	not to understand something correctly
miscalculate	to behave badly
misprint	to calculate wrongly
misunderstand	to judge something wrongly
misuse	to make a printing mistake

Practice

Choose the prefix **mis** or **ex** to complete each word.

1. _____ pronounce
2. _____ it
3. _____ lay
4. _____ fire
5. _____ trust

6. _____ port
7. _____ pose
8. _____ tract
9. _____ cavate
10. _____ clude

11. _____ manage
12. _____ lead
13. _____ pand
14. _____ hale
15. _____ plode

Challenger

1. Find the **mis** or **ex** word hiding in each line.
   Write the words in your book. The first has been done for you.

a) a b c <u>e x c h a n g e</u> g h j m d e
b) m i s m i s p l a c e m i s v x z
c) z x c v b e x t i n g u i s h m s o
d) q w e r t y m i s d e e d u i p l
e) g m i s t a k e f d j s k l a p w m
f) c b x n e x c e e d v b t r e a c p
g) e x c s d f e x i l e a q w o t m r
h) k l a f e w y r m i s i n f o r m c
i) e x t e r m i n a t e p o i u y t r
j) a z e c t b a m i s c o n d u c t

2. Choose three **mis** words and three **ex** words from this page.
   Make up one sentence for each word.

So – what have you learned about the prefixes 'mis' and 'ex'?

Focus

A **prefix** is a **group of letters** that comes **at the beginning** of a word.
If we know what the prefix means, it can help us understand some words better.

I put **anti**freeze in the water to stop it from freezing.

| **anti** often means **against**. |

There was a **co**llision as the two cars met each other.

| **co** often means **together**. |

The writing made no sense. It was a lot of **non**sense.

| **non** often makes a word mean the opposite. |

Check it out

1. Copy the table below. Write the words in the box in the correct columns.

cooperate	nonsense	collection
antibiotic	non-member	coordinate
antiseptic	non-stop	anticlockwise

anti words	**co** words	**non** words
antibiotic		

Practice

Copy the sentences below. Choose a word from the box in the 'Check it out' section to complete each one.

1. I have a large _____ of stamps in my album.

2. The doctor gave me an _____ for my bad throat.

3. There was _____ music at the disco all night.

4. The driver tried to go _____ round the roundabout.

5. If you _____, it is easier to work together.

6. I didn't believe what the child said. It was _____ .

7. Disinfectant is a kind of _____ .

8. Someone who does not belong to the club is a _____ .

9. _____ means to fit things together smoothly.

Challenger

Use a dictionary to write a definition for each of these words.

1. antidote   anticlimax   antipathy

2. coincide   coagulate   coexist

3. nonconformist   non-essential   non-intoxicating

So – what have you learned about the prefixes 'anti', 'co' and 'non'?

Homonyms

Focus

A **homonym** is a word with the **same spelling** or **pronunciation** as another word, but with a very **different meaning**.

There was a **tap** on the door.   The lady turned on the **tap**.

Check it out

Draw pictures of the following things in your book and label them.

1. a) a **bat** that flies   b) a cricket **bat**

2. a) a jar of **jam**   b) a traffic **jam**

3. a) a **band** that plays   b) an elastic **band**

4. a) some **glasses** you wear   b) some **glasses** you drink from

5. a) a light **bulb**   b) a flower **bulb**

6. a) a **letter** you send   b) a **letter** of the alphabet

7. a) a finger **nail**   b) a **nail** you hit with a hammer

8. a) a **wave** on the sea   b) a **wave** of the hand

Objectives ~ to explore homonyms which have the same spelling but
multiple meanings
~ to explore how the meanings can be distinguished in context

Practice

Use a homonym from the box to complete each pair of sentences.

1. I stuck the _____ on the envelope.

I like to _____ my feet in muddy puddles.

2. I had to _____ to avoid bumping my head.

The _____ quacked loudly.

3. The _____ got stuck between floors.

The case was too heavy to _____ .

4. The girl gave the door a _____ to open it.

The _____ pulled the ship into harbour.

5. I drew a straight line with a _____ .

King Henry was a _____ of England.

6. The man lit the candle with a _____ .

The football _____ had to be called off.

> lift
>
> ruler
>
> match
>
> stamp
>
> tug
>
> duck

Challenger

Write two sentences for each homonym below. Make sure you
use each word in two different ways.

1. box

2. barge

3. fair

4. calf

5. hide

6. park

7. cub

8. fly

9. bridge

10. coach

11. stick

12. drive

13. nut

14. bear

15. junk

So – what have you learned about homonyms?

Unit 30 Things people say

Focus

We use lots of **common expressions** for lots of **everyday situations**.

Check it out

Copy the following expressions in your book. After each, say if it is a way of greeting someone (an expression of greeting) or of saying goodbye to them (an expression of parting). The first has been done for you.

1. Hello (an expression of greeting)

2. See you later.

3. Hiya!

4. Howdy.

5. How's it going?

6. Goodbye.

7. Good morning.

8. Bye.

9. Cheerio.

10. Wotcha.

Practice

Copy the table below. Write each common expression in the correct column.

> Sorry.

> Stop!

> Well done

> Look out.

> I beg your pardon.

> Keep it up.

> Beware

> Please excuse me.

> Take care.

> You're doing well.

> Don't do that.

> Good work

> Watch your step.

> A good try.

> Many apologies.

Warning	Apology	Encouragement
Stop!		

Challenger

Write down four common expressions for each situation below.

1. expressing surprise

3. expressing thanks

2. asking someone to be quiet

4. telling someone to go away

After each, write if you would say it to a teacher (T), your
friend (F) or a stranger (S).

So – what have you learned about common expressions?

Range of Books Available

Year 3 Sentence	Year 4 Sentence	Year 5 Sentence	Year 6 Sentence
Year 3 Word	Year 4 Word	Year 5 Word	Year 6 Word

Literacy Differentiation Word Level Year 3

First published 1999

Letts Educational, Schools and Colleges Division,
9–15 Aldine Street, London W12 8AW
Tel: 0181 740 2270   Fax: 0181 740 2280

Text © Louis Fidge and Ray Barker

Illustrations © Richard Duszczak, David Lock, Tim Oliver, John Plumb and
Ken Vail Graphic Design (Liz Bryan)

Designed by Ken Vail Graphic Design, Cambridge

British Library Cataloguing-in-Publication Data
A CIP record for this book is available from the British Library

ISBN: 1 84085 231 3

Printed in the UK by Bath Press Limited

Every effort has been made to trace copyright holders and to obtain their
permission for the use of copyright material. The authors and publishers would
gladly receive information enabling them to rectify an error or omission in
subsequent editions.

Letts Educational is the trading name of BPP [Letts Educational] Ltd